CW01086723

THE
POLICE SERVICE

REAL life GUIDES

Practical guides for practical people

In this increasingly sophisticated world the need for manually skilled people to build our homes, cut our hair, fix our boilers, and make our cars go is greater than ever. As things progress, so the level of training and competence required of our skilled manual workers increases. In this series of career guides from Trotman we look in detail at what it takes to train for, get into, and be successful at a wide spectrum of practical careers.

The *Real Life Guides* aim to inform and inspire young people and adults alike by providing comprehensive yet hard-hitting and often blunt information about what it takes to succeed in these careers.

Other titles in the series include:

THE ARMED FORCES

THE BEAUTY INDUSTRY

CARPENTRY & CABINET-MAKING

CATERING

CONSTRUCTION

ELECTRICIAN

ENGINEERING TECHNICIAN

HAIRDRESSING

INFORMATION & COMMUNICATIONS TECHNOLOGY

THE MOTOR INDUSTRY

PLUMBING

RETAILING

TRAVEL & TOURISM

WORKING OUTDOORS

WORKING WITH ANIMALS & WILDLIFE

WORKING WITH YOUNG PEOPLE

REAL life GUIDES

THE
POLICE SERVICE

2nd Edition

CAROLINE BARKER

Real Life Guide to The Police Service

This second edition published in 2009 by Trotman Publishing, an imprint of Crimson Publishing Ltd, Westminster House, Kew Road, Richmond, Surrey TW9 2ND

First edition by Dee Pilgrim published in 2005 by Trotman & Company Ltd.

Author: Caroline Barker

© Trotman Publishing 2009

Design by Nicki Averill

British Library Cataloguing in Publications Data
A catalogue record for this book is available from the British Library

ISBN 978-1-84455-196-5

Typeset by RefineCatch Ltd, Bungay, Suffolk

Printed and bound in Italy by LEGO SpA

CONTENTS

About the author vii

Acknowledgements ix

Introduction xi

Chapter 1 **Success story** 1

Chapter 2 **What's the story?** 5

Chapter 3 **Case study 1** 9

Chapter 4 **Tools of the trade** 13

Chapter 5 **Case study 2** 23

Chapter 6 **What are the jobs?** 27

Chapter 7 **Case study 3** 41

Chapter 8 **FAQs** 45

Chapter 9 **Case study 4** 51

Chapter 10 **Training** 55

Chapter 11 **Case study 5** 63

Chapter 12 **The last word** 67

Chapter 13 **Further information** 71

ABOUT THE AUTHOR

Caroline Barker is a professionally qualified Careers Adviser with many years' experience of providing careers guidance and counselling services to a wide range of clients. She has worked with school pupils, Apprenticeship trainees, college students, and adults seeking a career change.

Seeking a career change herself, she moved into working as a freelance writer and research consultant, specialising in the fields of careers, education, and training. In this capacity she has worked for various careers publishers, including Cascaid, VT Careers Management, AGCAS, and Lifetime Publishing, as well as the Sector Skills Council Skillset.

Her work at present is predominantly geared towards young people. She is committed to producing accurate and engaging careers information for this readership, enabling them to make informed choices about their future career.

Caroline is a full member of the Institute of Career Guidance, a member of the Careers Writers' Association, an affiliate member of the Institute for Learning, and a conference member of AGCAS.

ACKNOWLEDGEMENTS

Many thanks to all the case study interviewees who gave up their time to discuss their careers and offer their honest opinions: PCSO Kathryn Bean of North Yorkshire Police; PC Nick Storey of the British Transport Police; Inspector Anthony Bedeau and Student Officer Sarah Hussain of West Yorkshire Police; Superintendent Mike Cloherty of Merseyside Police; and Julie Spence, Chief Constable of Cambridgeshire Constabulary. Hopefully I've conveyed their positive outlook and passion for their jobs within their case studies.

INTRODUCTION

Police and thieves, cops and robbers, the Bill and the bad guys: whatever we choose to call them, it seems the British public is obsessed with law enforcement officers and the criminals they set out to catch. Bands sing songs about them, authors write best-selling books about them, actors clamour to play them in films, and if you turn on the television on any night of the week you'll be able to tune in to a programme about the police. It seems that the men and women who operate within the criminal investigation system fascinate us all.

For a lot of people that attraction and fascination is all about what they see as the 'glamour' of the job: the smart uniforms, fast car chases, the arrest of dangerous, perhaps famous criminals, and the subsequent high-profile court cases. But this is only a tiny part of what being a member of the police service is all about. In fact, the police play a much more important role in society than simply chasing villains. They are there to serve the community by protecting life and property, by preventing and investigating crime, by prosecuting offenders, and by preserving order. People actually feel safer when they see 'bobbies' on the beat as their physical presence can decrease the risk of crime.

The police are there at the scenes of serious accidents, helping to keep traffic moving, comforting the injured and their relations, and taking eyewitness accounts of what has happened. You will find them wherever there are large gatherings of people, such as sporting events and marches, maintaining public order. If you are burgled or physically assaulted the police will investigate the crime, while on Friday nights and at weekends they are on hand in large city centres to curtail drunken disorder. These are just some of the more visible roles taken by over 140,500 police officers in England and Wales, but the police often perform their duties out of the public eye – investigating international drug gangs, detecting serious fraud such as money laundering, guarding against terrorist attacks, and even protecting important members of state. No wonder we are so interested in what they do.

Traditionally, the visible face of the police has been male and white. Now, in the same way as the country is moving towards a fully integrated multi-racial and multi-religious society, the make-up of the police service has changed. According to the Home Office, of those 140,500 police officers, 24% are female and 4.1% are from minority ethnic backgrounds. The service is recruiting more and more people from all ethnic and social backgrounds and people from all communities are keen to join.

The decision to become a police officer is not something you should take lightly. You need to think long and hard about whether this is something you really want to do. Although there are plenty of positive aspects to police work – the great variety in

NATIONAL ASSOCIATION OF MUSLIM POLICE (NAMP)

NAMP was launched in 2007 to be the first national representative body of Muslim police officers and police staff within the service. It seeks to:

- ▶ promote recruitment, retention and progression of Muslim police officers and staff
- ▶ support the welfare and religious needs of its members
- ▶ promote an understanding of Islam within the police service and the wider community, thereby contributing to community cohesion.

There are currently ten constituted and three interim Muslim police associations set up across the country.

Source: NAMP website www.namp-uk.com

the work, good pay structure, and opportunities for career progression – there are also the downsides, such as having to work shifts and the possibility of physical and verbal attack. Policing is a serious job, so you have to be serious about wanting to do it. The rigorous police tests you have to undertake when applying are there to weed out those who are not emotionally, mentally, or physically equipped for the job.

DID YOU KNOW?

According to the Home Office, 50% of all crime is committed by just 10% of offenders. And the most active offenders in the country are estimated to be responsible for a staggering one in ten offences.
Source: Home Office

But what skills and personal qualities help you to be a successful police officer? Even more important, what would becoming a police officer mean to you personally in terms of career development and financial benefits? This book is here to help you decide whether policing is really for you. It will explain exactly what a police officer is and what he or she does. It will also give you a better idea of the great variety of positions within the police service and what specific skills you need for them. Real life case studies will show you what serving officers actually think about their jobs. Finally, it will explain what the police recruitment process and training entails.

Reading this book will give you a better understanding about the police and policing and help you to make an informed decision about joining the force. Not everyone has the right mental attitude or personal qualities to make a success of a career in the police, so read on to discover whether or not you are one of those who do. Read the case studies thoroughly, as they will give you an insight into the person behind the job, and the attitude and personal qualities that have helped them succeed. Common themes are determination, enthusiasm, and the desire to develop their careers. Other themes are facing challenges, working in a job where every day is different, and the motivation to make a difference. They also give useful tips for someone thinking about joining.

CHAPTER 1
SUCCESS STORY

JULIE SPENCE
Chief Constable – Cambridgeshire Constabulary

As the Chief Constable for Cambridgeshire Constabulary Julie Spence has a dual role. She is responsible for ensuring fair and equitable policing services for people in Cambridgeshire, through the management of a service business employing 2,500 people with a budget of £125 million. This involves managing every department, from major crime to neighbourhood policing. She is one of five women chief constables out of 43.

After graduating with a degree in biology and physical education, Julie first trained as a teacher before becoming a police officer. She has been in the police service for 30 years.

'I wanted to work in the public service, in a helping profession. I've always had a commitment towards trying to improve people's lives and make a difference.'

Julie joined under the normal recruitment process and early on unsuccessfully applied for the accelerated promotion scheme. Undeterred she continued to progress and climbed the ladder nonetheless. She gained experience in a number of different departments, including uniform patrol, community policing, the Criminal Investigations Department (CID), and the family and child protection unit, whilst working her way up through the ranks. She joined Cambridgeshire in 2004 as Deputy Chief Constable responsible for operational policing and became Chief Constable in December 2005. In 2006 she was awarded an OBE (Officer of the Order of the British Empire) in the Queen's 80th birthday honours list for her contributions to British policing.

Julie always knew she wanted to become a senior manager and believes personal motivation is the key to achieving your goals.

'The chance that you'll be plucked out from a crowded street and made into a star is very rare. It's about what you're prepared to do, both in and out of work, in terms of advancing your learning and development, and broadening your experiences. The wonderful thing about the police service is that there are so many different opportunities to develop your career.'

In terms of her own development she has taken three degrees during her career (on a part-time or distance learning basis), in law, police studies, and management.

Throughout her career Julie has been committed to maximising the potential of all staff, including those in a minority. She has championed the cause for gender equality within the police service and has been instrumental in taking forward the Gender Agenda (which aims to make women feel valued and encourages their career development) and the development of the British Association for Women in Policing (BAWP). She is currently the President of the

○ DID YOU KNOW?

The BAWP was set up in 1987 and is the only organisation in the UK to embrace women of all ranks and grades within the police service. Its main objective is to enhance the role and understanding of the specific needs of women within the police. Source: www.bawp.org

BAWP, and also a leading light in the Association of Senior Women Police Officers.

In terms of her own force, Cambridgeshire run a full range of professional career development opportunities for staff. This also includes separate personal development programmes for men and women, as it has been shown each have different needs and approaches to personal development. Julie also works with the Association of Muslim Police and the Black Police Association with the aim of encouraging their members to take up opportunities, as well as providing mentoring schemes for individuals. Julie is also committed to increasing diversity in her force. She recently launched a recruitment campaign using equal opportunities legislation in order to recruit police community support officers (PCSOs) with language skills. The result is that there are now 25 languages spoken amongst PCSOs, serving a diverse community that incorporates 93 different cultures.

Julie is very positive about her job:

'I like everything about my job. Every day is a different challenge, whether it's a management challenge, a people challenge, or an operational policing challenge. I really like the fact that this was a failing force when I arrived and now we are among the most improving forces in England and Wales. It's about developing the people into part and parcel of a successful organisation. People now feel proud to be part of this organisation.'

The police service faces many different challenges.

'At the top end there is the terrorist threat. Then there is the increasing complexity of the world, for example, the use of the internet as a source of crime. Then there's the dimension of being a multi-cultural society, and looking at levels of understanding between police officers and different groups in society. The police service has to keep up with the ever-changing world. A big challenge at the moment is the victimisation of youth by the media. The number of bad stories written about young people in the media isn't proportionate to their misbehaviour but it does affect the public's perception. So as a force we're looking at ways of positively engaging with young people, and trying to get the public to put young people into perspective. The aim of policing is to have cohesive communities rather than alienated ones.'

The main skills and qualities a police officer needs, Julie believes, are 'integrity, respect, sensitivity (i.e. emotional intelligence), and common sense. Anyone working in public services will need a level of humility in order to understand others, as well as impartiality to deal with a situation fairly. It's also really important for anyone who is a police officer, whether a constable or a chief, to have leadership skills as they will always have to be able to negotiate in difficult circumstances or situations. The public will always look for the cavalry coming over the hill, and when the police arrive they will expect them to take charge.'

Julie's advice to someone looking to become a police officer is:

'When you feel you're ready to go for the interview process then go for it. Don't hold back. If you get turned down because you don't have enough life experience, then listen to the feedback, develop yourself further, then try again later. Also think about becoming a special constable or join as a PCSO, or as another member of police staff.'

And, for getting on:

'Seek guidance from a manager, or a career development officer. Think about what you can do to develop in your current role. Take responsibility for your own career.'

CHAPTER 2
WHAT'S THE STORY?

The days of the friendly local bobby in uniform walking slowly down the street, stopping to say 'evening all' to everyone he meets may seem to belong to a bygone age, but much of what police do now is the same as when the blueprint for our modern police force was first set up nearly 200 years ago. That was when Home Secretary Sir Robert Peel set out to overhaul and reform the penal code (i.e. the codes concerning punishment of criminals), giving rise to Britain's first 'bobbies' or 'peelers'.

Because we've all grown up with a properly maintained and trained police service it's almost impossible to believe there was a time when the police did not exist, although the people of Britain have had systems for keeping law and order since Saxon times. At that time a 'tithing-man', responsible for a group of ten people, had to answer to the Shire-reeve (Sheriff) of his shire or county if any of the group caused unrest. This system gradually evolved over the years until tithing-men became parish constables who were elected annually to serve (unpaid) for a year, while the Sheriff became the Justice of the Peace.

As the population of Britain grew, so too did the size of towns and the amount of crime being committed in them. So parish constables evolved again, this time into the 'Watch', who were paid for guarding the town gates, patrolling the streets at night and even lighting streetlamps. However, the beginning of the 18th century and the Industrial Revolution saw the populations of our towns and cities soaring and it became clear that a properly coordinated force to uphold law and order was needed. In 1742 London got the Bow Street Runners, although soldiers were still being used to quell riots and mass disorder. It wasn't until 1829 that the Metropolitan Police Act was passed and the first of Peel's police were seen on the streets of London. At first there were just 1,000 policemen, who were paid 16 shillings (80 p) a week and were based at Scotland Yard. To join, you had to be 6 feet (1.83 metres) tall with no history of any wrongdoing and be prepared to work 7 days a week.

After initial resentment and distrust from the public, these forerunners of our modern police soon proved their worth. However, it still took some time for other areas around the country to get their own forces – by 1855 there were only 12,000 policemen in the whole of England and Wales. In 1856 Parliament mandated that all provinces had to establish police forces and also made provision for government inspection, audit, and regulation of those forces. The era of modern policing had truly begun.

There are now 43 police forces across England and Wales, made up of a wider, extended police family than just police officers. Although special constables (specials) have been around for over 150 years, the Police Act of 1964 really established the Special Constabulary in its present form and now every force in England and Wales has its own Special Constabulary, with over 14,000 serving specials – who are unpaid volunteers – in total. A newer development has been the introduction of police community support officers (PCSOs) as a result of the Police Reform Act 2002. PCSOs provide assistance to the police but do not have full police powers. According to the Home Office there are currently over 15,000 PCSOs.

The police service believes that modernisation is essential to fight 21st-century crime and has been undergoing reform for a number of years. The aim is to reduce public fear of crime and build public confidence. At the heart of the proposals for reform is a drive to increase neighbourhood policing, providing a visible local presence, and to make sure the police service listens to the needs of individuals and local communities. The government White Paper

'Building communities, beating crime' (2004) set out proposals under which all forces were to implement Neighbourhood Policing by 2008. A mixed team of dedicated police officers, PCSOs, and special constables, who will be known to their community, now polices every neighbourhood.

The police service is committed to continue developing its work in terms of engaging with communities, which is outlined in the Policing Green Paper (July 2008) 'From the Neighbourhood to the National: Policing our Communities Together'. A vital part of building up the trust of the community is that the police service reflects the diversity (i.e. the 'difference' across race, gender, disability, sexual orientation, faith, and age) of the society it serves. To this effect, police forces are recruiting more and more people from all ethnic and social backgrounds, and as a result are becoming more diverse.

Home Office figures show that as of 31 March 2008 there were 237,114 full-time staff working in the 43 police forces in England and Wales. Of these, roughly 60% are police officers, 7% are PCSOs, and 32% are other civilian police staff. The make-up of the police has changed drastically from the traditional white six-foot

POLICE SERVICE FACTS

▶ The Metropolitan Police encourage staff to register their knowledge and/or membership of a community, languages spoken, life-skills obtained as a result of ethnic origin, sexual orientation, race, religion, and hobbies.

▶ The Greater Manchester Police have introduced a childcare voucher scheme to help staff balance work and childcare responsibilities.

▶ South Wales Police use gay officers to break down barriers between police and attendees at Cardiff's Gay Pride event.

Source: Home Office

male police officer. Women now comprise 24% of police officers, and 12% are working in the more senior ranks of Chief Inspector and above. Amongst officers, 4.1% are now minority ethnic officers (compared with 2.0% in 1999). The Metropolitan Police has the largest proportion of minority ethnic officers, at 8.2%.

Today the duties of officers are much more varied than they would have been during the Victorian era, but the first of Sir Robert Peel's Nine Principles of Policing still holds true. It says that 'the basic mission for which the police exist is to prevent crime and disorder'. Add to this protecting life and property, taking statements, arresting suspects, giving evidence in court, supporting victims, and even having to inform relatives about the deaths of crime or accident victims, and you can see just how demanding the role of the modern police officer is. However, it is also very rewarding because as a police officer you really can make a difference to society as a whole. Whether you are walking the street, giving a talk in a school, or maintaining order at a football game, members of the public know they can approach you for anything from asking for directions to getting assistance if they have been assaulted.

You need to be really committed to make a good police officer and you also need special skills and talents. For many people the shift working pattern of the modern police and the responsibilities of being an officer prove too much. However, this does not mean there is no place for them within today's police service. In Chapter 4 we look in more detail at what being an officer actually entails and the kind of strengths and abilities that can help you to make a successful career in the police, and in Chapter 6 we will discuss in detail the wide range of jobs available in the police service.

DID YOU KNOW?

The National Black Police Association (NBPA) was officially formed in 1998. Its main objective is to promote good race relations and equality of opportunity within the police services of the UK and the wider community.
Source: www.nbpa.co.uk

CHAPTER 3
CASE STUDY 1

KATHRYN BEAN
Police community support officer (PCSO)

Kathryn Bean works as a PCSO for North Yorkshire Police. She is based in York, in the York South Safer Neighbourhood Team.

The aim of the Safer Neighbourhood Team is to work with the community and other agencies to reduce crime and the fear of crime in the neighbourhood.

'My role is to make people feel safe. As a PCSO I'm there to reassure the public, as a high visibility police presence to deter crime. My job is to be the eyes and ears of the street and to gather intelligence within the community which I can feed back to the Intelligence Unit. I'm also there to be a friendly face. Whilst I do enforce laws on a daily basis, such as parking or cycling offences, a lot of my time is spent helping people.'

An important part of Kathryn's job is building up relationships – with schools, businesses, community groups, and residents in the area. She attends a monthly ward meeting where people living in the ward can raise issues that are concerning them, for example, problems with parking, speeding, or litter. Crime issues are also discussed. These could relate to burglaries, cycle theft, or anti-social behaviour. She also has a lot of contact with professionals from other agencies, such as youth workers and social workers, with the aim of helping young people who may be causing anti-social behaviour. She has built up relationships with local primary schools and regularly gives lessons on issues such as bullying, personal safety, and road safety.

Kathryn works shifts, normally 8am to 5pm or 1pm to 10pm, in a rota of three earlies followed by three lates. She mainly works on her own, but is paired up with another PCSO after 6pm. She has the reassurance, however, that in a local team another colleague will never be far away and her police radio acts as a lifeline. The police constable in her team who oversees her work is always available if she needs any assistance, for example, if she is detaining a suspect (which she can do under certain circumstances for up to 30 minutes). Kathryn spends a lot of time patrolling her area either on foot or on a bike. 'You definitely need to be fit to do this job!'

Her working day always starts with a briefing on incidents that have recently happened, and suspected criminals to watch out for. The rest of the day could involve being on patrol, in between various meetings and visits. If there has been a burglary, for example, Kathryn will visit the victim in their home to give crime prevention advice on how to make the property secure, and may also make house-to-house enquiries on neighbouring properties to gather intelligence. The job is also unpredictable and she could suddenly be called out to assist at an incident.

'If a crime scene needs preserving, I'll stand at the scene to prevent people going past and reassure the public. Or if there has been a road traffic collision I may be called out to point duty and be diverting traffic.'

Kathryn enjoys the unpredictable aspects of the job.

'Every day is a challenge, as you don't know what to expect. You could come across anything at any moment and need to be ready to deal with it.'

She also enjoys building up relationships with people.

'I've only been in this team since July but I've already got to know the local shopkeepers, social workers, and school teachers. I like talking to people and helping people. I like being busy!

Communication skills are essential. You need to be very tolerant and very resilient. Life experience helps, as it gives you experience of dealing with situations. You come across things that can be quite shocking so you also need to remain professional at all times. You can't let your emotions take over.'

Kathryn had always wanted to join the police service and put an application in to become a PCSO when she was 18 years old, but was told she needed some more life experience. After taking a horticulture course she was working as a florist when she decided to apply again and was successful. She has been a PCSO for around 18 months. She spent 4 weeks on a training course (for new recruits it is now 8 weeks), covering theory such as the powers PCSOs have and the laws they use, and physical training in the use of force and self-defence. Training is ongoing and varied, covering issues from increased powers of PCSOs to major incident training. Kathryn would like to further her career by becoming a police officer. Ultimately she would like to progress into a specialism, either within the dogs or mounted section.

Kathryn's advice to someone who wants to become a PCSO would be:

'Get some work experience in a job where you're dealing with people. Teamwork is important, as well as general life skills which you can gain, for example, through sporting activities.'

CHAPTER 4
TOOLS OF THE TRADE

This chapter focuses on the variety of skills needed to work within the police service. You could start by finding out if your idea of what a police officer is and does is realistic. Take a few minutes to do the quick quiz below to see just how much you really know about the police. Once you've done that, have a look at the list of the main skills, abilities, and personal qualities that are important to a career in the police. Some of these you will already have and some you may need to develop further if you decide that a career in the police service is the career for you.

QUIZ

Because we see police officers on the streets and in television programmes and films almost every day, most of us think we have a pretty good idea about what they do, how far their powers go, and what makes good police practice. In reality, however, it's surprising just how little we actually do know. The following quiz is a fun way to test your knowledge of the police. The early questions are fact-based, whereas the later ones look at how you would react in certain situations and whether or not that reaction is appropriate. This will give you a better idea of whether you have what it takes to make a success of a job in the police. After each question just tick the answer you believe to be correct.

1 **Who was the founder of the police service?**
A. Sir Bobby Peel.
B. Sir Robert Peel.
C. John Peel.

2 **What is the minimum age requirement to join the police?**
A. 17.
B. 18.5.
C. 21.

3 **Which of the following is not standard police issue?**
A. A baton.
B. A firearm.
C. CS spray.

4 **What is the major challenge to a police officer in today's society?**
A. Terrorism.
B. Anti-social behaviour.
C. Violent crime.

5 **What is a police constable allowed to do that a police community support officer cannot?**
A. Search a vehicle.
B. Make an arrest.
C. Issue a fixed penalty ticket for a minor offence.

For questions 6–10, try to put yourself in the position of a police officer dealing with each of the situations described.

What would you do?

6 **You have been called to the scene of a car crash in which a young person has been injured. He is pronounced dead by the ambulance crew. The parents need to be informed. Do you:**

A. Get someone else to do it?

B. Say their son is in hospital but they'll have to ask the doctors how badly injured he is?

C. Explain quietly, calmly, and with sympathy what has happened, expressing your own sorrow at their loss?

---

7 **You are called to a robbery at a local petrol station. When you arrive the gang is just getting away by car; one of them looks like he may have a gun. Do you:**

A. Pursue the getaway car in your patrol vehicle, hoping to cut them off and catch them?

B. Pursue the getaway car but immediately call your control room for armed back-up?

C. Pursue the getaway car, call for back-up, saying you think one of them may be armed, and keep monitoring the situation until you can be sure whether a firearm is involved?

---

8 **You arrest a suspected thief who has a quantity of prescription drugs on him. As you move to confiscate them he tells you they are for a serious medical condition and he cannot be without them. Do you:**

A. Take them away anyway – they might be stolen?

B. Let him keep them – without them he could get seriously sick?

C. Consult the police doctor to see if it is safe to leave them with him?

---

9 **While out on patrol one day you are stopped by a local resident complaining about a gang of young kids causing a nuisance in the area. He points them out to you and it is clear they are acting in an anti-social manner. Do you:**

A. Tell them to clear off, warning them that if they return you'll serve them with an Anti-Social Behaviour Order (ASBO)?

B. Go over and talk to them, telling them their behaviour is not acceptable and getting their names and addresses for future reference?

C. Immediately serve them with an ASBO?

10 **There has been some vandalism at a row of local shops and one of the shopkeepers is very angry and threatening to take matters into his own hands. Do you:**

A. Tell him this is not a good idea and show him you are taking the matter seriously by talking it through with him and discussing crime prevention measures he could take?

B. Let him get on with it – the vandals are a nuisance to everyone in the area?

C. Immediately arrest him – this is a police matter and he must not be allowed to interfere?

ANSWERS

1. B. Sir Robert Peel was responsible for bringing in the Metropolitan Police Act in 1829, which saw the first police officers on the streets of London. The term 'Bobby' was an affectionate term for the early officers and comes from the shortened version of 'Robert'.

2. B. The minimum age is 18.5 years old, but if you are over 16 years old you can join the Police Cadets, which is a good way to see whether a job in policing suits you or not.

3. B. All police constables are issued with protective vests, handcuffs, a baton, and CS spray but they do not, as a matter of course, carry guns. Although people are seeing more armed police on the street, the UK in fact has one of only very few unarmed police forces in the world. In situations where an armed response is called for, a member of a firearms unit, specially trained in handling weapons, will be brought in.

4. A, B, and C. This is a trick question! There is no one major challenge. Our modern police service is continually adapting and responding to changes in today's society and the problems associated with this. The ultimate challenge is to reduce crime and the fear of crime at all levels.

5. B. Unlike police constables, community support officers do not have the power of arrest. However, they can detain a person for up to 30 minutes pending the arrival of a police officer (this is similar to the power of 'Citizen's Arrest' which we all have). Another difference

between PCSOs and police constables is the equipment they carry: PCSOs wear uniform but they do not carry handcuffs, batons, or CS spray.

6. C. Having to inform families of victims about serious injuries and even deaths is part of the job of a police officer. This particular aspect of the job requires maturity and sensitivity.

7. C. When you become a police officer you have to accept that inevitably you will find yourself in potentially life-threatening situations. However, this does not mean you have to take unnecessary risks. Getting yourself killed while trying to be a hero (A) is just plain stupid, while calling out a firearms unit without good cause (B) is a waste of resources. A good officer would monitor the situation, keeping in contact with their control room at all times and requesting back-up as and when the need arises.

8. C. This question is based on a true-life situation, when an officer still on probation let an arrested man keep what he claimed to be prescribed medication. The man, a drug addict, then proceeded to swallow the whole bottle of pills, effectively overdosing and requiring a trip to hospital to have his stomach pumped. The man survived, but he could just as easily have died. When in doubt, ask someone who knows. In this case that would be the police doctor.

9. B. Telling a bunch of rowdy kids to clear off may make them move in the short term, but as soon as the police officers continue on their beat they are almost sure to return. Taking names and addresses means you can check up on them if their behaviour is a cause for concern in the future. Then, once they have been warned and have ignored the warning, the time is right to issue an ASBO.

10. A. The shopkeeper is obviously very distressed about what has been happening at his premises, but taking the law into his own hands is not the way to go. He needs your reassurance that you are taking his grievances seriously – you could do this by making detailed notes of the dates, times, and nature of the vandalism. He also needs constructive advice on how to stop the vandals – so talking through crime prevention measures (such as installing a CCTV camera) would be helpful. Sometimes, your job as a police officer may be to show your support by simply sitting and listening to members of your local community.

Count up how many of the above questions you got right. Questions 6–10 covered problem-solving and decision-making skills, both of which a good police officer needs. So, if you scored well on these, well done! The paragraphs below outline some of the other important skills, abilities, and personal qualities needed for a career in the police. Remember that what's important is not how much you know now but how much potential you have to develop these skills.

COMMON SENSE

You need to be methodical and accurate, so an ability to think logically is a must and this ties in with having a good deal of common sense. Many situations can be resolved by using a common sense approach.

COMMUNICATION SKILLS

Do you like to speak with people you haven't met before? Can you make yourself understood in a group of people who may not like what you have to say? If the answer is 'Yes', then you are already using the kind of verbal communication skills that a police officer uses. As a member of the police you will be talking to other officers and to members of the public all the time. You need to make yourself clearly understood. You may be talking to an elderly member of the public on the street, relaying information to your control centre via the radio, giving evidence in court, or giving talks to children in schools. What you say and how you say it matters and you will have to learn to adapt the way you talk depending on who you are dealing with.

Communication is not just about talking to people. You will need to have effective written and listening skills as well. If you want to improve your communication skills, then any kind of work experience that involves dealing with people will help.

CONFIDENCE

Self-confidence is a bonus whatever job you are going to do, but in the police service it's a must. For a start you need to be able to approach people from all walks of life, sometimes under threatening circumstances. Calming down a volatile situation becomes even harder if you feel intimidated yourself. You must also be confident in making decisions under pressure. The training for student officers will help to build your confidence, but you could improve it beforehand by challenging yourself to do something new. For example, learn a new skill, take up a hobby, or get involved with a school or community project.

MATURITY

Are you mature enough to cope with the pressures of the job? Do you have a wide enough experience of life? You will need to be able to stay calm under pressure, make decisions quickly, and use common sense. You will need to cope with vulnerable and injured people, and domestic and traumatic incidents. Maturity not only comes with age but through experience, so think about how you can widen your experience of life, for example, through voluntary work.

OBSERVATIONAL SKILLS

Court cases often rely on police evidence for prosecutions and so your powers of observation need to be strong. Exactly what colour was the shirt of the vandal you saw throwing that brick? What was the registration number of the stolen car in Long Road? Not only do you need to notice and remember facts and details, you also need to be able to record them accurately.

PATIENCE

Some cases take years to solve. Suspects must be eliminated, new evidence may come to light, and police officers will patiently have to sift through it all, building up a 'bigger picture' of the crime. You cannot afford to lose patience with a case, because this is when vital information can get overlooked, or the relevance of a statement can be missed.

PHYSICAL FITNESS

Your personal fitness is important not only to you, but also to your fellow officers. If a fellow officer is under attack, do you have the physical strength to help restrain the attacker? Do you have the stamina to work long shifts and encounter stressful and confrontational situations? More likely than not you will be out and about on your feet for most of a routine day and so a good level of health and fitness is essential. In fact, prospective officers must pass physical fitness and medical entrance tests before being accepted, as a certain standard of physical and mental health is needed to cope with the demands of the job. So if you are not involved with sports, think about getting fit another way, such as joining a gym, taking up running, or swimming!

RESPECT

The police are there to protect the whole of society, not just a chosen few, so good police officers are those who have respect for others' beliefs and points of view. Members of the community need to trust their police officers and be confident they will be respected and treated fairly. You will also need to be tolerant and impartial in all situations.

SENSE OF HUMOUR

This is one quality you might not have even thought about when considering the police as a career, but if you want this to be a job for life, you really do need to keep a sense of humour. You will be dealing with serious issues every day, and if you feel you are not making headway against crime and disorder it can really get you down. You need to be able to laugh and to keep a sense of perspective to stay motivated.

TEAMWORK

Although you should be able to show you can work independently using your own initiative, you really have to be a team player to be a member of the police. This means building good working relationships with your fellow officers and ensuring you are functioning as a unit. People need to know they can rely on you when things get tough.

OTHER THINGS TO CONSIDER

Honesty and discipline are also important qualities to have within the police service. Any form of prejudice (including racial, gender, sexual orientation, and religious) will not be tolerated within the police, nor will an inability to follow orders from a superior officer. Also, if you have any sort of criminal conviction, even for something you think is quite trivial, you must declare it when you apply to join the police. There are some convictions that will immediately make you unsuitable for the job, and don't think that you can get away with it by keeping quiet – you will always get found out!

Now you've read about the qualities you need to make it in the police, you are probably realising just why it takes an induction course and a further two years of training before a constable is fully qualified. If you decide that becoming a police officer is not for you, there are still many other roles within the police service you may be suited to. There are positions for everybody, whatever their abilities and interests. In fact, the huge variety of job opportunities available is one of the reasons many people join the police force in the first place. In Chapter 6 we look at the range of roles available.

CHAPTER 5
CASE STUDY 2

NICK STOREY

Police Constable – British Transport Police

Nick Storey is a response officer with British Transport Police (BTP). He is based at York railway station, which lies on the East Coast Main Line – on the main route between London and Scotland. York is a district within the north east area of BTP that covers most of North Yorkshire.

Nick's main role is the detection and prevention of crime in and around the railway, with the aim of reducing crime and the fear of crime on the railway system. Like any other uniformed police officer, part of Nick's job is to provide a high visibility police presence to reassure the public.

He works on shifts, normally alongside another response officer but not always.

'A typical day might start by arriving at 7am, dealing with any prisoners from the night before, and then progressing any enquiries in order to investigate crimes. This could involve taking witness statements from an alleged victim of assault or gaining CCTV footage of suspects.'

Once he starts a case it is his responsibility to gain the evidence, construct a file, liaise with the Crown Prosecution Service, and ultimately progress the case to court if there is enough evidence.

Nick receives a daily briefing on ongoing crimes or people wanted for crimes. He also receives information from the Intelligence Department or another BTP office for him to act upon. If, for example, a luggage thief has been sighted on a train in Darlington heading towards York, Nick would then meet the train coming in and make an arrest.

Nick enjoys the variety and challenges of working for BTP.

'I love the job! Every day is different. As a specialist force we could be called to literally anything. One minute I could be assisting an elderly lady with her luggage across the road, the next I could be called out to a fatality on the railway. Flexibility and adaptability are therefore important skills. Also at York we are pretty much self-managed. If a supervisor isn't on shift we have to think on our feet and make decisions for ourselves. It's also important to be approachable, have good communication skills, and an inquisitive nature.'

Crimes and incidents on the railway vary from common offences such as assaults, drunk and disorderly, and theft, to more complex situations such as murders, train crashes, and terrorist incidents. Fatalities are not uncommon. If Nick is called out to a fatality on the line, this involves attending to the scene, recovering the body, identifying the person, and then passing on the news to the next of kin, possibly all on one shift. He then has to deal with the incident right through from filing the initial report to going to the coroner's inquest.

His patch is not confined to York but covers the majority of North Yorkshire. He may have to make an immediate response to a theft of railway cable on the line somewhere in rural North Yorkshire to search for suspects, or he could be called out to a violent incident on the railway in Scarborough and have to search the crime scene. The job also involves train travel, for example, escorting large numbers of football fans back home after an away match. Also, as he works for a national force, he may be called out of his area to assist at a major incident. In 2005 he spent two weeks in London carrying out prevention-of-terrorism stop searches because the terrorist threat was so high.

Nick had always wanted to be a police officer and had previously applied but not got in. He was working as a landscape gardener when he joined BTP as a special constable. Two years later he was successful in his application and went on to complete his two-year probationary training period, which included training at the Police Training School, post-foundation courses on legislation covering firearms and sexual offences, and on-the-job training based in York. Since then he has received training in anti-terrorism search, crime scene search and CBRN (chemical, biological, radiological, and nuclear) response. He is a trained response driver, which means he can respond to emergencies. He is looking to take his sergeant exams in the near future and would like to move into a supervisory role. In the meantime he is very happy where he is.

Nick's top tips for someone wanting to become a police officer would be:

'Good verbal and written communication is vitally important. Also, a good educational background would assist, especially in subjects like English and any foreign languages. Computer skills would advantage someone, and physical fitness, of course, is critical.'

CHAPTER 6
WHAT ARE THE JOBS?

In this chapter we focus on who does what in the police service. The bobby on the beat and the police community support officer within your local community may be the most common faces of the police you see in everyday life, but they are by no means the only roles the police play. As we saw earlier, there are dozens of different jobs in law enforcement, each needing different skills and abilities. Some you may already be familiar with, but others may be quite new to you. Take a look at the different departments available within the police force and the different specialised roles available to police officers; the roles of specialist police forces; and examples of police staff (civilian) jobs working in departments at the heart of the police resolving crimes.

POLICE OFFICER

Since the first days of the peelers, police officers have been responsible for maintaining law and order, investigating and preventing crime, and bringing criminals to justice. Uniformed police officers carry out their duties in a variety of different ways and in many locations. They may be out on patrol or they may be working in front of a computer, or giving a talk in a school. Some days they may be drafted in to police special events such as football matches or rock concerts.

They are usually assigned to an area, which they patrol either on foot or in a marked police car. Police officers aim to reduce crime in their community. They play a crucial role in protecting the public from crime and anti-social behaviour, providing support to the victims of crime and working with other agencies to reduce crime.

Police officers may conduct searches; attend incidents such as burglaries and traffic accidents; arrest and interview suspects and take statements; charge offenders; and give evidence in court. To become a police officer you must be 18.5 years old or over and pass rigorous medical and fitness tests before completing a two-year training period.

For more information see the Could You Police? website (see Chapter 13).

DID YOU KNOW?

In 2007/08 1 in 5 (22,151) offences of attempted murder, grievous bodily harm, and robbery involved knives or sharp instruments.
Source: British Crime Survey (England and Wales)

Many officers love the variety of being on the beat so much they choose to remain there for their whole career. However, others decide to receive further training in order to have a specialised role within a specific area. These are described below.

CRIMINAL INVESTIGATION DEPARTMENT (CID)

The CID investigates serious crimes such as murders, serious assaults, robberies, fraud, and sexual offences. Detectives working for CID are plain-clothes police officers who are ranked within the normal police hierarchy, e.g. detective constable, detective sergeant. Detectives investigate crimes reported by the public or businesses. They gather evidence, arrest suspects, interview them, and, if charges are brought, prepare case files. Complex enquiries involve a lot of analysis, problem solving, and paperwork, and so you must be able to pay great attention to detail in order to be a successful detective.

Uniformed officers must complete their two-year training period before they can be considered for any post within the CID. They can then apply for the post of trainee detective. Selection is competitive, and many police officers gain valuable experience by spending a few weeks on CID attachment before applying. Within the CID you could be working in one of the following specialist units.

The major crime unit

You could be an experienced officer working for the major crime unit investigating a high-profile murder enquiry, operating out of dedicated major incident rooms. These enquiries are complex and lengthy. Some officers in this unit are specially trained to work as family liaison officers, responsible for supporting the families of homicide victims, a demanding but important role.

The fraud squad

Fraud, especially credit card and internet fraud, is one of the areas where criminal activity has mushroomed in recent years and increasing numbers of officers are now employed in tackling it. You could be an officer in the fraud squad dealing with complicated fraud cases, especially those involving banks and organisations dealing with investments and money. Many officers who work in the area of fraud have very specialised computer skills.

The drug squad

Criminal dealings in drugs have increased greatly in recent years and now many officers are involved with tracking down drugs entering this country and keeping dealers under surveillance. Some drug squad operations involve forces from overseas as well as those in the UK and may take months to set up. Drug squad officers may concentrate their efforts upon organised drug dealers, but also assist officers who deal with the illegal possession and misuse of drugs.

DID YOU KNOW?

Fraud costs the economy an enormous amount: a report commissioned in 2007 by the Association of Chief Police Officers (ACPO) estimated the cost of fraud to be at least £13.9 billion a year.
Source: The Home Office

Child and public protection unit

Working in this unit you may be investigating cases of abuse against children. The unit also investigates people who are using the internet to distribute abusive or indecent pictures of children. They also investigate reports of domestic abuse and serious sexual crime such as rape, and provide support to victims. Police officers working in this unit are specially selected for their skills in dealing with complex and sensitive crime, and receive specialist training.

DID YOU KNOW?

Global profits from people smuggling are estimated to be US$10 billion annually. There are around 400 organised crime bosses in the UK with an amassed criminal wealth of approximately £440 million.

Source: Home Office 2004, *One Step Ahead: A 21st Century Strategy to Defeat Organised Crime*

THE SERIOUS ORGANISED CRIME AGENCY

The Serious Organised Crime Agency (SOCA) was formed from the former National Crime Squad in 2006 with the aim of tackling organised national and transnational crime. It is an agency with law enforcement powers sponsored by the Home Office. It supports CID in dealing with professional criminals operating across force and national/ international boundaries. Detectives investigate organised crime such as drug trafficking, people smuggling, and money laundering.

SPECIALIST OPERATIONS/ COUNTER TERRORISM

Specialist Operations within the Metropolitan Police Service houses the Counter Terrorism Command, which is tasked with protecting London and the UK from national security threats. It acquires and develops intelligence on terrorism and extremism, provides specialist security advice, and provides a bomb disposal and CBRN (chemical, biological, radiological, and nuclear) capability in London. Specialist Operations also houses Protection Command with units that provide armed personal protection services for public figures and members of the royal family.

Counter terrorist officers are fully trained police officers with additional skills and training. They also work at seaports and airports, and forces now also have counter terrorism security advisers who identify sites in their area that may be vulnerable to terrorist attack and devise security plans to protect the local community.

ROAD TRAFFIC DEPARTMENT

The Police Traffic Department isn't just concerned with catching speeding motorists. Road policing officers deal with a variety of incidents, such as vehicle crashes, pedestrians injured by vehicles, checking the safety standards of cars on the roads, and also delivering road safety education. They attend all potentially life-threatening collisions and provide support to CID for major incidents such as murder investigations. You would receive specialist training, and need to pass an advanced drivers course. You may be riding a motorbike or driving a police car.

DID YOU KNOW?

There are now in excess of 300,000 recorded injuries and approximately 4,000 deaths on the British roads each year. Source: www.westyorkshire. police.uk

POLICE SUPPORT UNIT

Police support units provide a range of specialist services in addition to high visibility core policing, and can be brought in to different areas at short notice to assist local officers. This could be to police football matches or demonstrations, or to assist in large scale operations such as missing persons searches, or looking for murder weapons or evidence in a large area. They also provide other services, such as an initial response to suspect explosive devices. Experienced officers who join receive specialist training, for example, in dealing with petrol bombing, and in house entry and search. You may also work within one of the following specialist units:

Air operations unit or underwater search unit

You may work within the **air operations unit** as a trained air observer in a force helicopter, helping a unit on the ground to chase a stolen car or a suspect on foot at night. Or you may work within an **underwater search unit** as a qualified police diver, to recover bodies, property, and drugs from lakes, canals, and rivers.

Police dog unit

Police dog handlers work together with their dog as a team. Each dog lives at home with its handler and usually retires as a family pet. You may be called upon to assist in missing persons searches and hostage situations. Some dogs are trained to find specific scents, such as drugs and explosives, hidden firearms, or human remains. They are also skilled in disarming violent armed suspects and controlling hostile crowds. Each force only needs a limited number of dog handlers at any time, however, so competition for places as a dog handler is fierce. You would follow a structured training scheme.

Firearms unit

Authorised firearms officers are professionally trained in the use of firearms. They are called in to assist in specific, and potentially very dangerous, circumstances such as hostage situations or when armed members of the public are proving a danger to other civilians, the police, or both. You would receive in-depth training for this demanding job and will need to be in top physical shape.

Mounted police unit

Mounted officers play a vital role at events where there are large crowds and where it is important to show people that there is a visible police presence. They may also be called in to cover large areas, such as open moorlands, in the search for a crime suspect. They are also involved in community policing, for example, visiting schools. You would follow a four-month training course and need to pass a riding test and written examination covering all aspects of stable management. You would then be allocated a regular mount, which allows you to build a relationship with your horse.

SPECIALIST POLICE FORCES

The Special Constabulary

The Special Constabulary is the UK's part-time police force. Each police force has its own Special Constabulary. It is made up of trained volunteers who work with and support their local police. Specials, as special constables are known, come from all walks of life and volunteer a minimum of four hours a week to their local police force, forming a vital link between the regular police and the local community. Once they have completed their training, they have the same powers as regular officers and wear a similar uniform. There are 14,000 specials serving with police forces across England and Wales.

Specials carry out duties alongside their regular colleagues. Duties may include dealing with anti-social behaviour, providing security at major events, conducting house-to-house enquiries, carrying out vehicle checks, and presenting evidence in court. Foot patrols and patrolling in a vehicle, in order to provide a police presence, will normally take up over half your duty time in the specials.

Although not paid a salary, specials are reimbursed for their expenses. Volunteering as a special gives you a chance to give something back to the community whilst learning new and useful life skills. It is also as a great way of learning first-hand about the police force before deciding to apply for jobs there. Many specials go on to train to become police officers. To find out more, visit the Could You Police? website (see Chapter 13).

British Transport Police

British Transport Police (BTP) is the national police service for the rail and tube network, providing a service to rail operators, their staff, and passengers. Every day they police the journeys of over 6 million passengers, covering over 10,000 miles of track.

The BTP is committed to building a safer railway environment. In the year 2007/08 the BTP dealt with over 70,000 crimes (including homicide, theft, and sexual offences), handled public order issues (such as overseeing large crowds of football supporters travelling to away games), and even handled suicides.

Its 2,835 police officers are recruited and trained in exactly the same way as those in local forces and have the same powers. However, they also receive specialist training in railway operations, safety, and legislation. As well as its officers, the BTP also has 259 police community support officers (PCSOs), 249 special constables, and 1,455 civilian support staff. More information can be found at the BTP website (see Chapter 13).

Royal Military Police

Royal Military Police (RMP) are commonly known as Redcaps because of their eye-catching headgear. The RMP is the branch of the army responsible for policing the army both in the UK and abroad. They provide a military police presence on service property (at garrisons) and support the military on operations. They also specialise in criminal investigations.

To begin a career in the RMP you must first join as a soldier. You need to be at least 17.5 years old, and preferably have GCSEs in English and Maths at grade C. After successfully completing your basic military training (normally 12 weeks), you can go on to complete your specialist training, a 21-week military policing course at the RMP training school in Chichester. You then become a lance corporal.

There are plenty of opportunities for promotion or for going into specialist areas such as Special Investigations Branch (the army's equivalent of the CID). There are also great opportunities for travel, as the RMP force is based all over the world. If the disciplined life of a soldier appeals to you and you like an occupation with plenty of physical activity (there are opportunities to learn to ski, sail, parachute, and mountaineer within the RMP), then this could be the job for you. You can find more information on the Armed Forces websites (see Chapter 13).

POLICE STAFF (CIVILIAN) JOBS

The police service offers many front-line crime-fighting operational roles for which you don't need to be a police officer. These police staff (civilian) jobs are at the heart of crime detection, investigation, and law enforcement. You would be working alongside police officers and serving the public whilst developing your skills. You could be working in a number of different departments, teams, or units.

Neighbourhood policing team

Police community support officers (PCSOs) are police support staff employed within neighbourhood policing teams, working alongside other police officers. The role was introduced after the Police Reform Act 2002 and, with the increasing emphasis on community policing, their numbers have been rising ever since. There are currently 13,400 PCSOs in forces across England and Wales.

They contribute to the policing of neighbourhoods mainly through high visibility patrol (wearing distinctive uniforms), reassuring the public, and dealing with local problems like anti-social behaviour. The priority of the role and the powers required to fulfil it are about making the public feel safer and reducing the fear of crime. PCSOs have powers to deal with anti-social behaviour, alcohol and tobacco offences, some minor parking obstruction offences, and in some forces the power to detain someone until a police officer arrives. PCSOs wear a uniform and work on shifts.

Working as a PCSO is an ideal way of gaining experience if you're considering a career within the police force, and many PCSOs go on to train to become police officers. For more information visit the Could You Police? website (see Chapter 13).

Intelligence unit

The gathering of intelligence is seen as one of the most important elements in mounting operations against the professional criminal. **Crime analysts** collect and analyse patterns of crime, using specialist computer software and technology. They study information from various sources such as the media and force information systems trying to identify trends, offenders, and crime groups. They may specialise in areas such as serious organised crime or anti-terrorist activities. Applicants increasingly have first degrees or postgraduate qualifications, and criminology is a particularly useful subject.

Hi-tech crime unit

Crimes using computers are rapidly increasing and range from computer hacking and online fraud to drug dealing and pornography. In this unit **forensic computer analysts (FCAs)** or **hi-tech crime investigators** specialise in computer crime, or cyber crime. They collect and analyse evidence from computers, even if it has been deleted or corrupted. Their work includes stripping down hardware, accessing hard-drive data, and internet investigations. Some FCAs are police officers with specialist computer training; others are computer specialists working as support staff. Most FCAs have a degree in IT or another computer-related subject. There are degree courses that specialise in forensic computing.

Criminal justice support department

The police need paralegal support in case management and initial preparation of cases for prosecution. You may work as a **case builder**. After being given the initial case papers by police officers, you would prepare the file for submission to the Crown Prosecution Service, by obtaining the statements, and medical and forensic evidence. Legal training is offered for these posts.

Custody section

You may work within the custody environment, as a **detention officer** assisting the custody officer in the detention of prisoners/detainees. Detention officers attend to the welfare and security needs of people in custody. This job is a people-based role and requires a caring attitude. Duties may also include taking photographs, fingerprints, DNA samples, and administration.

Scientific support department

When any crime has been committed, the investigation of the crime scene is always the starting point. Anything left at a crime scene, such as fingerprints or DNA samples (found, for example, under hair or in fingernails), can be used to help solve crimes and prosecute suspects. Forces have police staff who specialise in this type of work. You could be working in a number of units; these are described below.

Crime scene investigation

Crime scene investigators (CSIs), or **scenes of crime officers (SOCOs)**, attend crime scenes such as murders and car crime to record and examine evidence. The evidence CSIs discover is then used to investigate crimes. Duties range from dusting for fingerprints and taking photographs of accidents to searching an area for footwear marks and examining surfaces for samples such as fibres and blood. They send fingerprints and other items to internal police laboratories for chemical analysis. Samples such as fibres, blood, and other body fluids are sent to an external forensic laboratory for analysis. This profession is very popular and is becoming increasingly graduate-level entry.

Fingerprint bureau

Fingerprint officers search and compare finger and palm marks from crime scenes against a national fingerprint database in excess of 6 million people. They can also take fingerprints from detainees and search against the national database of crime scene marks. The fingerprint bureau can even identify criminals through their footprints, which are also unique. Some fingerprint experts are also trained in handwriting analysis.

Digital imaging unit

The extensive use of digital cameras, CCTV cameras, mobile phones, and other forms of capture device means that there are now more opportunities for detecting crime aided by imagery than ever before. **Imaging officers**, working with digital cameras or video cameras, may attend a serious crime scene or road traffic accident to complement the photographic work of the CSI. They then produce photographs of fingerprints and footprints to help identify the owner of the marks. **CCTV analysts** work with CCTV images to bring out the highest quality of detail possible from poor quality images.

Secretarial and administrative staff

Secretarial and administrative police staff work in departments across the whole service, from media and marketing to human resources and finance, making sure the service runs smoothly on a day-to-day basis. Examples of jobs include **clerical assistant, personal assistant, and legal typist.** For these positions some form of secretarial experience will be needed before joining the force. Other positions include **communications/control room officer**, answering 999 calls and directing officers to incidents; **crime recording personnel**, recording crimes onto the crime system and ultimately the police national computer; and **front counter personnel**, manning the front counter and answering queries.

As you can see, a great variety of roles are available within the police service, so there's probably a niche somewhere for your own particular skills and abilities. Take a look at the Who Does What and Where Chart (Figure 1) to see where you may fit in.

FIGURE 1
THE POLICE: WHO DOES WHAT AND WHERE

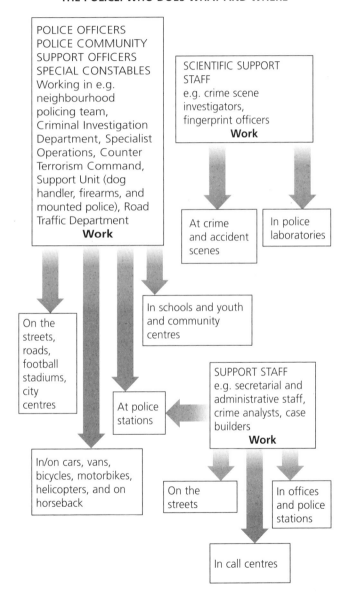

CHAPTER 7
CASE STUDY 3

MIKE CLOHERTY
Superintendent

Superintendent Mike Cloherty works for Merseyside Police. He is in charge of operational policing for the Wirral area, the second biggest policing area in Merseyside. He has been in this post for a year.

'I am responsible for making sure we deliver the policing services to the satisfaction of the community and the police authority. This covers all the uniform and CID resources and [police] officers in the Wirral, including 700 members of staff, delivering a police service to 330,000 members of the community across an area of 60 square miles.'

He is part of a policing team that has to meet targets set by the government on crime reduction, crime detection, reduction of anti-social behaviour, and satisfaction of users. Satisfaction targets, relating to the quality of service provided, are a recent development:

'We take into account the needs and expectations of the various communities we work within. The community has a greater voice now.'

On a typical day, Mike will arrive in the office at 7.30am and start looking at the various crimes and incidents that have taken place in the last 24 hours. He will go through the statistical data and look to see if they are staying below targets. He will then meet with various chief inspectors and agree the priorities for the day. If, for example, there has been a high number of robberies, he will task someone with concentrating on this particular issue. This may involve a marketing campaign to warn residents of robberies in their area, or working with the local authority to improve the use of CCTV cameras.

The day will continue with attending various meetings addressing key issues, for example, how they are using their budget and how they are performing in relation to targets. Mike also has meetings with external agencies involved with community safety, such as social services, to make sure that the policing services complement services provided by other agencies. He stresses the importance of not just reacting to certain situations, such as a child murder, but learning from them for the future.

Mike will deal with and coordinate an emergency response to incidents that happen during the day in the Wirral. He also does 60 days in the year (60 shifts of 9–10 hours) when he is on cover as the senior officer for the force responsible for providing an emergency response to any major incident, for example, a firearms incident or a fire. Mike is also involved in planning and delivering the policing operations at a number of high-profile events, such as the Tall Ships Race this year, which saw over a million people visiting Liverpool.

Mike is also the lead for Merseyside Police on knife crime and is involved, along with 10 other police forces, with the Home Office project 'Tackling Knives Action Programme'. In a bid to reduce knife crime the project funds police forces to tackle knife crime in a number of different ways, from educational programmes in schools with the aim of preventing the use of knives, to running operations using portable safety arches as a means of detecting knives.

'A really positive aspect of this initiative has been the creation of youth forums in every policing area in Merseyside, developing links with young people in order to gain a better understanding of their views and experiences regarding knife crime.'

Having always had an interest in the work of the police, Mike started his career with Merseyside Police at 21 years old, looking for something more varied than the civil service office-based job he was in. He has stayed with Merseyside, and moved to the operational support division early on, where he was trained in bomb search and public order management. After that Mike studied for and passed his sergeants exams, and then his inspectors exams, in order to progress through the ranks. After becoming an inspector Mike took the national police leadership training course and has since gone on to complete a degree in Police Leadership and Management, studying part-time at Liverpool Hope University.

Mike has worked as an inspector in charge of planning major public events, as well as working as a neighbourhood inspector, then chief inspector, in the Croxteth and Norris Green area of Merseyside. Here he developed work in the community to deal with the increasing problem of gang factions. This led him to take a four-month secondment to the Home Office on the 'Tackling Gangs Action Programme' in 2008, before being promoted to his present position.

Mike is passionate about all aspects of his job:

'I can honestly say I love everything about it. I love the variety and unpredictability of working in operations and events. I also get to meet some really interesting people, from different backgrounds, and get to work with various organisations. It's the biggest privilege I've had to do this job.'

Mike's top tips for someone wanting to become a police officer are:

'Make sure you get the best qualifications you can in school, as entry is becoming more competitive. Make sure your CV looks better than someone else's. Get involved in youth groups, community work, volunteering. There are also opportunities to get involved in the cadets, or as a special constable.

The main skills needed are communication, problem solving and, above all, common sense with a sense of proportion. Other areas which are seldom mentioned in job descriptions are energy, enthusiasm, and a positive outlook.'

And, for getting on:

'Get involved, show that you're keen and take advantage of the training available. It's a fantastic career, with different experiences and opportunities available. There's no other job like it!'

CHAPTER 8
FAQs

By now you should have a much better idea of what joining the police is all about and the wonderful opportunities it can offer. The detailed descriptions of the different positions within the police may help you to decide where you would eventually like to end up in the service, but what about the everyday conditions on the job? What will becoming a member of the police force mean to you financially and socially? Even more importantly, how will it affect your future career prospects? In this chapter we look at some of the most commonly asked questions about getting a job within the police and the benefits it can bring to you personally. This should help you to decide whether or not this is a career path you wish to follow.

Q **Am I eligible to apply to become a police officer?**

A You can apply to be a police officer from the age of 18, although you will not be appointed until you reach the age of 18 years and 6 months.

You must be a British citizen, a European Community/European Economic Area (EC/EEA) national, or a Commonwealth citizen or a foreign national with no restrictions on your stay in the UK, but you must have been resident for more than 3 years.

Your application will be rejected if you have been convicted or cautioned for serious crimes such as rape or murder. You may be eligible if you have minor convictions or cautions, but there are many occurrences that may lead to a rejected application, so if you are unsure check with the force recruiting office as to your eligibility. A search for any criminal convictions or cautions will also be made against your family.

You cannot play an active part in politics (for example, by standing to be an MP) or be a member of the British National Party or similar organisations whose aims and objectives contradict the promotion of race equality and diversity. This is seen as a conflict of interests.

The conflict of interest rule also applies if you, or your spouse or a relative living with you, has a business interest in the area of your force (say a shop, a gambling shop or a business licensed to sell liquor such as a pub or off-licence).

If you have any visible tattoos that are viewed as inappropriate and could be offensive to members of the public or colleagues (e.g. a swastika) this could stop you from becoming a police officer.

See Chapter 10 for details on the application process.

Q **Are there good opportunities for promotion?**

A Yes, there definitely are, because the higher ranks are filled from within the force itself. Everyone has equal opportunities, and motivated and progressive people will receive training and encouragement at every stage in climbing the promotional ladder. There is a defined structure for this. In order to progress from the rank of constable to sergeant, and then from sergeant to inspector, you must first pass a qualifying examination. Inspectors seeking promotion can take the Core Leadership Development Programme. Chief inspectors, superintendents, and chief superintendents can follow the Senior Leadership Development Programme. Selection for chief officers (assistant chief constable, deputy chief constable, chief constable) is through the Police National Assessment Centre. Successful candidates take the Strategic Command Course, which trains them for the most senior ranks.

Once you've successfully completed your two-year training period you will be eligible to apply for one of the many diverse job opportunities available within the police service. Whether it's aiming for promotion or looking to specialise, you can begin to shape your own career. Fast track opportunities are also available for a limited number of police officers through the High Potential Development Scheme. See Chapter 10 for more details on training.

Will I work 9am to 5pm?

Definitely not! Police officers work unsocial hours, including early morning and late night shifts. Although a standard working week is 40 hours with two days' rest, police officers are usually expected to work a repeating shift pattern that provides 24 hours emergency cover, 7 days a week, 365 days of the year. You will also be expected to work overtime to provide support as and when needed, for example, at planned operations such football matches. Many police officers, especially student officers, find this a useful way of boosting their pay packet.

 What are the holidays like?

This varies between forces, but student officers may receive 22 days leave per annum, rising to 25 days after completing their training period. This then rises incrementally depending on your length of service, and may rise to 30 days after 20 years. Female officers are also entitled to maternity leave, and male officers may be entitled to paid paternity leave. In some circumstances police officers can take what is known as a 'career break' of up to five years. This is discretionary – it will depend on your police record and is a matter for your chief officer to decide.

 How much can I expect to earn?

Policing is a serious job with many serious responsibilities and the pay structure reflects this. The figures below from the Police Federation of England and Wales are based on salaries that were introduced in September 2008, as part of a 3-year pay settlement for police officers. When you first undertake your training the salary is around £22,104 a year, rising to £24,675 on completion of initial training (usually about 6 months), and then to £26,109 on completion of 2 years' service as a constable. Year on year your salary will rise to a maximum of around £34,707 a year. This is also the initial salary for a newly qualified sergeant, whose pay can rise to £39,006 after 4 years. Obviously, the higher the rank, the higher the pay: inspectors earn from £44,469 for a newly appointed inspector, to £48,234 after 3 years. Chief inspectors can expect to earn up to £51,246. If you are working in London, then you will receive a London weighting – this is extra pay to off-set the higher living costs in the capital. For example, in London, inspectors' pay starts at £46,419 and rises to £50,199. If you're under the rank of inspector you can earn more by working overtime, but this will obviously depend on your individual circumstances.

In terms of police support staff, pay varies between forces. The following figures are therefore only a guide. PCSOs' salaries may start around £17,000 (with shift and weekend allowances this could reach around £22,000), rising incrementally to around £19,000. Communications officers may earn between £19,000 and £22,000, case builders between £17,000 and £21,000, and detention officers between £15,000 and £18,000. Crime scene investigators may have a starting salary of around £16,500, rising to £35,000 for senior crime scene investigators. Crime analysts may start around £17,000, rising to £42,000 for a senior analyst.

What about future financial security?

If future financial security is important to you, then it's worth knowing that the Police Pension Scheme is one of the few 'final salary' schemes still around. This means that the amount you get is a percentage of the salary you retire on, so you're not relying on the ups and downs of the stock market. Membership of the scheme is usually automatic when you become an officer, although you can choose to make other arrangements. You can even transfer pension contributions you have made from previous employment into the scheme. The monthly contribution rate is currently 9.5% of your gross salary (i.e. your pay before tax etc. is taken away) and a full pension is payable after 35 years' service.

Will I be able to choose where I work and live?

Where you work will depend on which force you choose to join. This may depend on where you currently live and what opportunities are available locally. Once you have joined a force you will be required to perform your duties anywhere within the area that force operates, so you could find yourself moving around within your specific locality. Or, in the case of the British Transport Police, which is a national force, you could be drafted in to help out anywhere in Britain. This degree of flexibility is one of the things many police officers actually like about joining the force.

You will also have the opportunity to move to other forces by applying for a transfer. You may, for example, wish to move from a small county force to a big metropolitan force in order to gain more experience, or wish to move areas because of family commitments. A successful transfer request will very much depend on whether the force to which you wish to transfer actually has any vacancies, whether you have the necessary experience to fill that vacancy, and your length of service. In terms of working abroad then, there are limited opportunities. Specialist officers may be involved in training police forces in other countries, and occasionally officers may travel abroad in connection with cases they are working on. These, however, are exceptions to the norm, unless you work for the Royal Military Police, in which case you could be posted virtually anywhere in the world.

Q **What can I expect to get out of the job personally?**

A In short, some extremely professional training that will enable you to deal with all sorts of people and situations. This training will give you a sense of actually making a difference to the community you live in and the knowledge that ordinary people are reassured by your presence. From the little old lady who is anxious about going to the shops, to the witness to a crime who needs your protection, the very fact that you are there in uniform and have sworn to preserve order and prevent crime is a major contribution to the sense of well-being in society as a whole. At the end of the day you can feel a sense of pride that you are making a contribution to cutting crime and making our streets and roads a safer place to be.

Another added bonus is the camaraderie you experience with your fellow officers. Not only will you be spending a lot of time with them during working hours, but they are also the men and women you rely on for your safety during difficult situations, and friendships forged within the force can last a lifetime. Many forces have their own sports and social clubs (such as football, rugby, running, and tennis), so a social life in the police can be a rich and varied one.

 How will the public view me?

There will always be a section of the public that does not like the police, from people who just don't like authority figures to the persistent offender who frequently breaks the law. Doing this job you are never going to be everyone's friend, but on the whole the public will see you as enormously valuable. When law and order breaks down, the public looks to the police to take the lead and to restore the status quo. If you are mugged, your home is broken into, or your car is stolen, then the police are the first port of call. We look to them for reassurance, comfort, and protection. The public perceives the police as its guard against lawlessness and this is not a responsibility to take lightly.

CHAPTER 9
CASE STUDY 4

ANTHONY BEDEAU
Force Positive Action Officer

Anthony Bedeau is the Force Positive Action Co-ordinator for
West Yorkshire Police, based within the recruitment department in
Wakefield. His rank is inspector.

His role is to help form a diverse workforce, and was created as a
response to the Home Office setting targets for the recruitment of
black and minority ethnic (BME) police officers. He's been in post
for 3 years.

'I applied for this job because I wanted to make a difference.
I think it's important that we have a diverse workforce, that
represents the communities that we live in.'

Tony's job has had an impact – recruitment of BME police officers
has increased from around 2–3% to 6%.

Tony conducts and supports recruitment events, with a
particular focus on recruiting BME police officers. This may
involve attending job fairs, local events, and careers events in
schools, colleges, and universities. He works in partnership
with divisional training officers and external agencies such as
JobCentre Plus.

He provides advice, encouragement, and support both to people seeking a career within West Yorkshire Police (giving feedback, for example, to people who have failed the assessment centre) and staff already in the organisation. The aim is not only to recruit, but also to retain staff.

'I have contact with people through recruiting them, and afterwards, if they have any problems, I make sure I'm available for them to come and speak to me to try and resolve them.'

Tony runs workshops and seminars for people interested in applying to be police officers. Workshops involve a small group of up to 12 people, and will cover the specific recruitment process – looking at the application form and discussing what happens at the assessment centre. Seminars are larger groups and focus more on an overview of the organisation, but also cover the recruitment process. He covers aspects such as the different job roles available, structure of the force, conditions of service, and welfare and diversity issues.

The job is varied. One day he could be giving a talk to college students on a public service course, the next he could be sitting in a JobCentre Plus office helping unemployed people to fill out their application forms. He helps people who are applying for police staff roles too, such as clerical, IT, or call-handling vacancies.

Tony has enjoyed a varied career within the police force since joining after university.

'I had some friends in the force who encouraged me to apply, so I did and got in. I joined the Metropolitan Police and got a good grounding as a PC before applying for a transfer to West Yorkshire Police. I went on to be a training and development officer at the force training school, where I was involved in delivering diversity training. I was then promoted to police sergeant of a patrol team in Leeds before moving to Wakefield, where I was a police sergeant with responsibility for community safety, dealing with areas such as schools and housing. I worked as a temporary police inspector in a patrol team before being promoted into my present job.'

Tony is involved in targeted recruitment campaigns. He keeps a list of people who have shown an interest and contacts them before a recruitment campaign starts, inviting them to a seminar. In the last recruitment campaign, 12% of applicants to police officer posts were BME, as were 11% of applicants to PCSO posts.

The job is very people-based. 'Communication skills are very important. Also being approachable and friendly, as I'm here to listen, try to help, and assist.' Positive aspects of the job are when Tony sees someone he has worked with being successful in their application and starting in post. It can be frustrating, however, when people are unsuccessful, and it is out of his hands, for example, if they fail the medical or the vetting.

Tony's top tips for someone wanting to become a police officer are: 'Get as much information as you can – talk to police officers and look on the internet – to find out about the role. You'll need to show examples of your skills during the recruitment process, as past performance is a good indicator of future performance. Get some work experience, and aim to improve your communication, planning, and problem-solving skills. This could be anything from working in a shop to doing some voluntary work in the community.'

CHAPTER 10
TRAINING

So now you've really decided that joining the police force is what you want to do, what's the next step? This chapter discusses the recruitment process and the training programme you will follow as a student officer. Finally it looks at some courses you may be interested in finding out more about.

RECRUITMENT PROCESS

First you must check you are eligible (see Chapter 8). If you are, what qualifications will you need? There are no set academic requirements for entry into the service, although some forces may ask for specific grades at GCSE in certain basic subjects (e.g. English/maths). Entry, however, is becoming more competitive. Whilst you don't have to be a graduate, many people do join after taking a degree. All prospective candidates have to pass the Police Initial Recruitment Test (or the Scottish Police Standard Entrance Test in Scotland). Some forces may ask for a full driving licence or require you to learn within a specific time period.

First you must decide which force around the country you want to join, as you can only apply to one force at a time. You can check out which forces are currently recruiting on the Could You Police? website (see Chapter 13). Then go to the force website recruitment pages for details on how to apply. A number of forces have developed Pre-Recruitment Access courses running at local colleges to help would-be candidates, or may offer recruitment information sessions.

If your application is successful you will be given a date to attend an assessment centre. Here you will undergo a variety of exercises designed to reflect performance. Exercises include a competence-based structured interview, a numerical reasoning test, a verbal logical reasoning test, two written exercises, and four interactive (role-play) exercises. After you've passed your assessment you will be given appointment times for an eyesight test, a medical examination, and a fitness test. You will also be asked for references and you must pass a security check. Only when you have passed all of these will you be offered a place as a student officer on the 2-year Initial Police Learning and Development Programme (IPLDP).

DID YOU KNOW?

Somewhere between 60,000 and 80,000 candidates apply to join the police service each year, but only 8% are successful.

Source: Join the job website www.Jointhejob.com

INITIAL POLICE LEARNING AND DEVELOPMENT PROGRAMME

The IPLDP was introduced in 2005 in a move to professionalise the police service and its training. It was drawn up by the Home Office, and is designed to prepare officers for the demanding role of policing in 21st-century Britain. Forces now have responsibility for delivering their own training programme at a local level. You may be training at headquarters, an external training facility, a college, or even a university. There is also an increased emphasis on community engagement. This is to make officers more effective in their communities when they arrive.

Many forces require student officers to work towards NVQs at Level 3 and 4 in policing in order to complete their IPLDP and be confirmed in post. Alternatively, an increasing number of forces now require their student officers to successfully complete a Foundation Degree in Police Studies. This gives students an externally recognised qualification from which they can advance to further study. The structure and content of the IPLDP varies between forces, so you will need to contact your local force to find out what programme they run. Below is an example of the IPLDP in practice.

Induction period

Here you will be introduced to the force, and given more information as to what your 2 years as a police officer will be like. This may be around 3 weeks.

Community placement

Over 2 weeks you will gain an understanding of the importance of working with local communities.

Initial training

This consists of around 18 weeks of training on legislation, procedures, and guidelines. This may be achieved through a combination of classroom-based training and practical exercises. You will learn about the law and the core skills an officer needs to deal with a whole range of different police procedures. You may receive public order training, witness and suspect interview training, and search techniques. There may now be some time off for annual leave.

Tutored phase

This is where you get to meet the public face-to-face. Working with a trained tutor constable you will be allowed out on patrol, putting what you have learned into practice. The tutor constable is there to help and advise you with any queries or difficulties you may have. Whilst dealing with real events you will be assessed as to your suitability for independent patrol. This normally lasts around 8–10 weeks.

Independent patrol

Once you are judged fit for independent patrol you can head out on your own for the first time. This doesn't mean you are

FIGURE 2
CAREER OPPORTUNITIES

PASS POLICE INITIAL RECRUITMENT TEST

TWO-YEAR TRAINING PERIOD AS STUDENT OFFICER.
PROGRESS TO CONSTABLE

EXPERIENCE ON JOB AND MORE TRAINING
ROAD POLICE TRAFFIC DEPARTMENT
SPECIALIST OPERATIONS/COUNTER TERRORISM
SPECIALIST OPERATIONS/COUNTER TERRORISM COMMAND
CRIMINAL INVESTIGATION DEPT
POLICE SUPPORT UNIT (dog unit, mounted police, firearms unit)

GAIN MORE
EXPERIENCE
AND TRAINING

HIGH POTENTIAL
DEVELOPMENT SCHEME.
GAIN POSTGRADUATE LEVEL
QUALIFICATIONS AND FAST TRACK
PROMOTION OPPORTUNITIES
THROUGH RANKS

TAKE EXAM TO BECOME SERGEANT

GAIN MORE EXPERIENCE AND TRAINING.
TAKE EXAM TO BECOME INSPECTOR

GAIN MORE EXPERIENCE AND LEADERSHIP DEVELOPMENT
TRAINING. PASS SELECTION PROCESS TO BECOME CHIEF
INSPECTOR, SUPERINTENDENT, AND CHIEF SUPERINTENDENT

GAIN MORE EXPERIENCE AND SENIOR LEADERSHIP
DEVELOPMENT TRAINING. PASS SELECTION PROCESS TO
BECOME CHIEF OFFICER, i.e. ASSISTANT CHIEF CONSTABLE,
DEPUTY CHIEF CONSTABLE, AND CHIEF CONSTABLE

alone; you will be part of a team. You may be attached to a neighbourhood police team or a response team. You will be monitored and assisted by your colleagues and supervisors throughout the rest of your two years.

Continued assessment

During the programme student officers are assessed against 22 modules (National Occupational Standards), and required to build a portfolio (Student Officer Learning and Assessment Portfolio). This catalogues your learning and development, both in the training establishments and the workplace. Once you have successfully completed the IPLDP, you will become a fully fledged police constable.

HIGH POTENTIAL DEVELOPMENT SCHEME (HPDS)

Once you're a newly trained police constable, there is a possibility of fast-tracking your career through the HPDS. This scheme is designed to develop talented people into police leaders of the future. HPDS officers on stage one of the scheme gain a qualification at postgraduate diploma level. Officers on stage two work towards a master's qualification. HPDS officers will normally be promoted to the next rank when they satisfy their chief officer that they are competent. This can speed up progression, as they don't have to wait for a vacancy to become available. The HPDS is currently being revised by the National Police Improvement Agency (NPIA), so check for up-to-date information on their website (see Chapter 13).

DID YOU KNOW?

In 2008 the National Police Improvement Agency (NPIA) received 369 applications for the High Potential Development Scheme (HPDS). Out of these, 84 officers were successful at meeting the required standard for entry to the scheme.
Source: www.npia.police.uk

Do bear in mind that higher-ranking officers are promoted from within the police service itself, so if you don't pursue the HPDS there will still be plenty of opportunities to move up the police career ladder by taking the necessary examinations. If that does not appeal, you can always move sideways by specialising in a specific branch of policing such as dog handling or the fraud squad.

RELEVANT COURSES/ PROGRAMMES

14–19 Diplomas

14–19 Diplomas combine essential skills and knowledge, hands-on experience, and employer-supported learning, to prepare young people for the world of work. The Diploma in Public Services is currently under development and will be available in some areas from 2010. The content of the Diploma hasn't been confirmed, but will include subjects like protecting society; leadership and management; fitness, health, and wellbeing; and strengthening communities. This diploma will provide another route for young people seeking a career in public services. This is not, however, a vocational qualification.

The Diploma in Society, Health and Development is currently available in some areas. It is not as directly relevant, as it covers the broad context of four sectors: children and young people; social care; health; and community justice. It does, however, provide a general awareness of the community justice system. Further information on these diplomas is available on the diplomas website (http://yp.direct.gov.uk/diplomas/).

BTEC National Diploma in Public (Uniformed) Services

A number of colleges offer this Level 3 qualification, which is an alternative to A levels for young people wishing to work in the uniformed public services. Entry requirements are four GCSEs, including English language, at grade C or above, or equivalent. Subjects include expedition skills, diversity, discipline, teamwork, and leadership. This course is full time for 2 years.

Foundation Degree in Police Studies

As mentioned earlier, some forces require their student officers to complete a Foundation Degree in Police Studies as part of their training. However, depending on where you live, it may now also be possible to complete the Foundation Degree in Police Studies before applying to join the police. Northamptonshire Police, Lancashire Police, Cumbria Constabulary, and police forces in the East Midlands have been working in partnership with local universities to develop and deliver such courses. So it is worth checking whether there is anything available at your local university.

These foundation degree courses are full time for 2 years, with flexible study methods. Entry requirements are usually one A level or equivalent, or alternatively your work experience may be taken into account. An important element of the course is practical, work-based experience as a special constable, and you may have to become a special constable before you enrol, or during your first year. Training is based around preparing for operational policing as well as covering topics such as criminal law and justice, policing in the community, introduction to forensic science, and criminal investigation. At the end of the course you will be an occupationally competent officer. You will, however, have to apply to join the police force through the normal recruitment process.

As you can see, the recruitment and training of a modern-day police officer has been designed to reflect issues within the 21st century. It is important to remember how periods of study, personal development, and/or work experience may help you before applying, and, once in the police service, how these same experiences can enhance your career development.

Read the next chapter to find out more about the experiences of a current student officer.

FIGURE 3
ACCESS TO: THE POLICE SERVICE

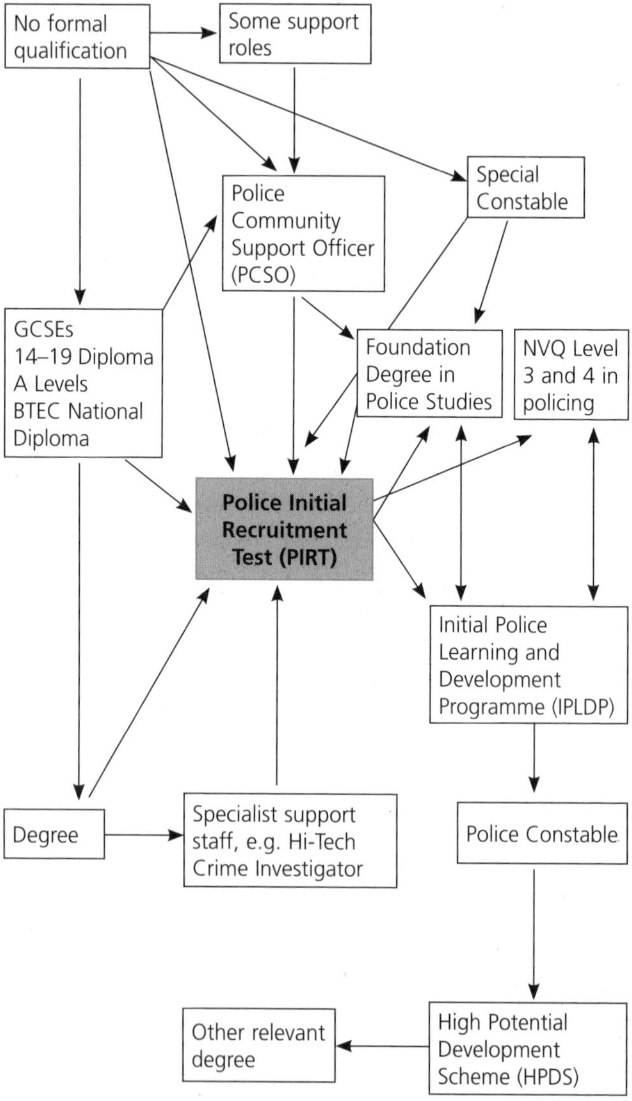

CHAPTER 11
CASE STUDY 5

SARAH HUSSAIN*
Student officer

Sarah is a student police officer with West Yorkshire Police and has so far completed 9 months of her 2-year training period to qualify as a police officer. She is working in a Neighbourhood Policing Team based in Leeds city centre.

Sarah was in the third year of her degree course when the police came in to the university to give a talk on joining the specials. This motivated her to apply to join the specials, but soon after recruitment opened for regular officers, she applied and got in.

'I wanted to help people and try to make a difference, which you really can do in this job. I also really liked the thought that every day would be different – and it is!'

All student officers in West Yorkshire Police gain their practical policing experience within a Neighbourhood Policing Team. The job involves a lot of contact with local residents, community groups, and agencies such as social services and youth offending services.

---

*Name has been changed

'I see my role as a helper within the community. Working at the heart of communities is integral to the future of policing. It's important to realise it's not all about whizzing about in patrol cars.'

Sarah works in a team of other police officers, PCSOs, and specials.

A typical working day?

'There isn't one! I could be on patrol, on the lookout for people who are wanted for arrestable offences, or who have breached their curfew or ASBO (anti-social behaviour order), or be attending a community meeting to listen to residents' concerns over nuisance behaviour and local crime. On one shift I could be called out to an incident involving domestic violence and make an arrest, on another I will be in Leeds city centre on a Friday night dealing with drunken fights.'

Sarah works a shift pattern – working earlies (7am to 3pm) and lates (5pm to 3am) in blocks of 7 days on and either 3 or 4 days off. When she comes on shift she'll be briefed on what's been happening – for example, burglaries or robberies that have taken place – and may be allocated a crime as part of her ongoing crime workload. She investigates crimes and has the role of gathering intelligence and submitting it to the court. This may involve taking a statement from a witness, making a house search, or trying to identify shoplifters caught on CCTV through using the police computer.

Sarah enjoys all aspects of her job.

'You meet so many different people in different circumstances and every situation is unique. You can help people from different backgrounds and cultures. I love my job. I even like the paperwork!'

She is passionate about trying to change people's perceptions of the police and feels that being friendly and approachable is an important aspect of community policing. What she does find frustrating is when members of the community feel that the judicial system is too lenient with offenders and then blame the police for not doing more, when they have actually done all they can.

Since starting in the job Sarah hasn't had to draw her baton or use her gas.

'Being able to calm situations down, talk to people, and reason with them is an important quality. You also need to be resilient as you witness a lot of things (substance misuse, sexual exploitation, child abuse – as well as negative attitudes towards the police) that could bring you down. It is also important to be impartial and accepting of people from all walks of life.'

Sarah has spent 4.5 months at Bishopgarth in Wakefield for initial training, including IT training and a day's public order training, as well as attending Huddersfield University for 4 weeks as part of her Foundation Degree in Police Studies. This course is a compulsory aspect of her training, and looks at wider social and community issues affecting policing. She will be fully qualified once she has successfully completed 2 years in training.

Once qualified, Sarah is considering either taking her sergeants exams or applying to be a trainee investigator within CID, and would ultimately like to move up the ranks.

'Currently there are no black and minority ethnic women police officers at the rank of inspector or above in West Yorkshire Police, so maybe I could be the first?'

Sarah first applied to join the police when she was 18, but was told she didn't have enough experience. By the time she applied again, she had worked in various jobs such as barwork and working in a call centre, which helped her application, as they were customer-facing roles. Sarah's top tips for someone wanting to become a police officer would be:

'Get a whole variety of life experience. Don't give up on anything you really want to do. If you don't get in the first time, apply again.'

CHAPTER 12
THE LAST WORD

If you've gone to the trouble of picking this book up in the first place, then you must have some interest in finding out what being a member of the police service actually entails. If what you have read has shattered any illusions you may have had about this being a glamorous and exciting career, that's probably a good thing: you'll now know that there is no place in today's police for people who want to speed about in fast cars, throwing suspects across their bonnets, and shouting 'You're nicked!' in a mockney accent. Policing is a serious business and if you want to join the police you have to be serious about it. That said, it is a richly satisfying and rewarding career that can make you feel you have really made a difference to the community around you. Not many jobs give you the opportunity to meet such a broad cross-section of society in such a wide variety of situations and locations. There's also plenty of opportunity for advancement either through promotion or simply by moving sideways into a different division.

You'll already have read about the different positions within the force and about other jobs associated with policing if you decide the challenges of being a police constable are not for you. If you are still determined to join the police, there are some practical things you can do while still at school, college, or university to increase your chances of being a successful candidate.

▶ Get a variety of life experience. Do some voluntary work, get involved in your local community, join some youth groups – whatever you do, get to meet people from lots of different sections of society. Aim to get some work experience where you are dealing with people and can improve your communication, planning, and problem-solving skills. Re-read the tips from the case studies.

▶ Join the Police Cadets. You can join from the age of 16 up until the age of 18 (and in some forces from 14). This will really give you an insight into what the police actually do, as well as the opportunity to serve your community. It will also give you the chance to talk to people who are already working in the police about what it is like. You normally attend weekly sessions at a police station, and may get involved in activities at the weekends or in the school holidays. There are lots of Police Cadet schemes around the UK, so contact your local force for details of their scheme.

▶ Attend a force open day. Many forces have open days throughout the year where you can go and talk to officers face-to-face about what their jobs entail. Not only will this give you a better overview of the police, but might also help you to decide which part of the force you would eventually like to specialise in.

▶ Learn to drive. Already having a full driving licence when you apply to join can be a bonus, and driving is a good life skill to have anyway.

▶ Become a police community support officer (PCSO). Although you will not have all the powers a police constable does, you will still be able to help maintain law and order and assist in many ways. This is a great way to gain experience within the service and see at first hand what the police really do. Further information is available on the Could You Police? website (see Chapter 13).

▶ Become a special constable (special). If you are working in another job but can spare at least 4 hours a week to work on a voluntary basis, then you could become a special. Again, this is a great way to gain valuable experience. See the Could You Police? website for further information (see Chapter 13).

▶ Become a volunteer. There are a number of voluntary roles available within the police service, from working as a front-line interpreter to helping witnesses or giving station tours. Forces have different needs, so contact your local force for details of opportunities locally.

SIR ROBERT PEEL'S NINE PRINCIPLES OF POLICING

1. The basic mission for which the police exist is to prevent crime and disorder.

2. The ability of the police to perform their duties is dependent upon public approval of police actions.

3. Police must secure the willing co-operation of the public in voluntary observance of the law to be able to secure and maintain the respect of the public.

4. The degree of co-operation of the public that can be secured diminishes proportionately to the necessity of the use of physical force.

5. Police seek and preserve public favour not by catering to public opinion but by constantly demonstrating absolute impartial service to the law.

6. Police use physical force to the extent necessary to secure observance of the law or to restore order only when the exercise of persuasion, advice, and warning is found to be insufficient.

7. Police, at all times, should maintain a relationship with the public that gives reality to the historic tradition that the police are the public and the public are the police; the police being the only members of the public who are paid to give full-time attention to duties which are incumbent on every citizen in the interests of community welfare and existence.

8. Police should always direct their action strictly towards their functions and never appear to usurp the powers of the judiciary.

9. The test of police efficiency is the absence of crime and disorder, not the visible evidence of police action in dealing with it.

Source: http://www.nwpolice.org/peel.html

Take the advice from Chief Constable Julie Spence: 'When you feel ready to go for the interview process, then go for it. If you get turned down because you don't have enough life experience, then listen to the feedback, develop yourself further, then try again later.' And from Student Officer Sarah Hussain: 'Get a whole variety of life experience. Don't give up on anything you really want to do. If you don't get in the first time, apply again.' Good luck!

If you've made it this far through the book, then you should know whether being a police officer really is the career for you. Here's a final checklist to see if you're the right person for the job!

Tick Yes or No

Do you have energy, enthusiasm, and a positive outlook?	☐ Yes	☐ No
Do you want a career that challenges you?	☐ Yes	☐ No
Do you have the stamina to work long shifts and encounter stressful situations?	☐ Yes	☐ No
Can you communicate effectively with lots of different people?	☐ Yes	☐ No
Do you want a job where you will be doing something different every day?	☐ Yes	☐ No
Do you have integrity, respect, and sensitivity?	☐ Yes	☐ No
Are you able to negotiate in difficult situations?	☐ Yes	☐ No
Do you have the ability to solve problems with a common-sense approach?	☐ Yes	☐ No
Are you friendly and approachable?	☐ Yes	☐ No

If you answered 'Yes' to all these questions, then congratulations! You've chosen the right career! If you've answered 'No' to any of these questions, then a career as a police officer may not be for you; however, there are still plenty of jobs within the police service that may suit you better, such as communications officer, detention officer, or administrative support.

CHAPTER 13
FURTHER INFORMATION

GOVERNMENT BODIES/ OFFICIAL WEBSITES

Could You Police? www.policecouldyou.co.uk

This is the official Home Office recruitment website for police officers, special constables, and PCSOs. It tells you everything you need to know about joining the police. You will find information on eligibility, what the jobs are like, how to apply, pay and benefits, and which forces are actually recruiting. The site also gives links to all police forces in the UK.

Home Office www.homeoffice.gov.uk/police

This comprehensive site has information about roles within the police service. It also gives an excellent summary of the role, structure, and strategy of police forces in England and Wales.

National Police Improvement Agency (NPIA) www.npia.police.uk

The NPIA provides products and services to support the work of police services. It is currently revising the High Potential Development Scheme.

Jobs4u www.connexions-direct.com/jobs4u

This website, funded by the Department for Children, Schools and Families (DCSF) is aimed at 13- to 19-year-olds and gives excellent information on jobs and careers. Click on the A–Z of Occupations and you will find job descriptions and specifications for the police and related fields.

Prospects www.prospects.ac.uk

This is the official graduate careers website, where you can explore types of jobs through an A–Z search.

Learndirect www.learndirect.co.uk

This site has been set up for adult learners and it has an excellent job profile section where you can find detailed descriptions of hundreds of jobs. It also gives a realistic indication of what salary structure is like and links to other, related sites.

Skills for Justice www.skillsforjustice.com

Skills for Justice is the sector skills council involved in the development of the following 14–19 Diplomas: Diploma in Public Services, and Diploma in Society, Health and Development. General information on diplomas, and up-to-date information on developments is available on their website.

UNOFFICIAL WEBSITES

Specials www.policespecials.com

This website has information on joining the Special Constabulary, and a members' forum where potential new recruits can ask questions and get answers from serving officers. It also has information on law and procedures.

Police Community Support Officers (PCSOs) www.national-pcsos.co.uk

At this site you can really get a feel of what it is like to be a PCSO: it gives news, views, and updates on policy and actual individual Community Support Officers' experiences.

Police Information
www.police-information.co.uk

This is an information resource for the policing and law enforcement community and covers information on news, laws, procedures, the recruitment process, careers, and salaries.

Join the Job www.jointhejob.com

This site is packed with information about how to join the police service as a police officer.

Bluelinecareers www.bluelinejobs.co.uk

This is a job site dedicated to police staff recruitment. You can conduct a job search and view current vacancies.

Police Oracle www.policeoracle.com

This site is a resource for UK police services, and includes information on careers as well as vacancies in the police service.

POLICE SUPPORT GROUPS

British Association for Women in Policing (BAWP) www.bawp.org

The BAWP actively works to promote the role of women within the force.

National Black Police Association (NBPA) www.nbpa.com

The objective of the NBPA is to promote good race relations and equality of opportunity within the police service.

National Association of Muslim Police (NAMP) www.namp-uk.com

The NAMP is the national representative body of Muslim police officers and Muslim police staff.

Gay Police Association (GPA) www.gay.police.uk

The GPA offers advice and support to gay police service employees.

SPECIALIST POLICE FORCES

Royal Military Police (RMP) – British Army
www.army.mod.uk

Information is available on this army website.

British Transport Police (BTP)
www.btp.police.uk

This official site gives information on the history and role of the British Transport Police. It has a comprehensive recruitment section covering different roles, how to apply, training, and career development.

Ministry of Defence Police (MDP)
www.modpoliceofficers.co.uk

The MDP is a specialised national force that operates within the defence community. This official site explains the role of the force, and has information on career opportunities and how to join.

Civil Nuclear Constabulary (CNC)
www.cnc.police.uk

This official site has information on the role of the CNC, an armed police service dedicated to the nuclear industry. It has information on career opportunities and vacancies.

FORENSIC SCIENCE SERVICE

www.forensic.gov.uk

This site gives an introduction to the work of the Forensic Science Service, a leading supplier of forensic science services to the UK police. Click on the Careers section of the site for detailed information on qualifications, duties, ways to train, and even work experience opportunities. In this section there is also a Vacancies site.